THE

JELLYFISH

DREAM

POEMS BY

VARINIA A.
RODRIGUEZ

PUNCH DRUNK PRESS LTD | | DENVER, COLORADO

For information, address:
Punch Drunk Press Ltd.
PO Box 9435
Denver CO 80209
Interior Design: Brice Maiurro
Cover/Back Cover Photography: Varinia A. Rodriguez
Cover Design: Brice Maiurro
Rodriguez, Varinia
The Jellyfish Dream / Varinia A. Rodriguez 1st Ed.
ISBN – 978-0-9988902-5-8

Note from the Author

I'd like to thank Connor Marvin for once asking me what I believed jellyfish dreamt about by telling me they had brains. They don't, but the suspension of facts and reality birthed a magical way of looking at life to make sense of it all.

I'd like to thank Michelle Martinez for gifting me the book, "Women Who Run with Wolves," by Clarissa Pinkola Estés. It brought me closer to magic and healing.

And most importantly, I'd like to thank Brice Maiurro for constantly pushing me to write and inspiring me with his dedication to poetry.

This book is an exploration of feelings and not reality. The search for truth and sincerity, through dreams and metaphor. The sentiments are the reality. The reality being the process of eight years of growing.

Thank you for all the people that impacted me to get here.

PUNCH DRUNK PRESS

PUNCH DRUNK PRESS LTD
DENVER CO

TABLE OF CONTENTS

The Jellyfish Dream

"What do you think
jellyfish dream about?"
He asks.

"Some jellyfish
have eight brains
and when they sleep
seven shut down
while one brain
keeps them moving.

Does each brain
dream the same thing
or
do they have their
own dreams?"

I tell him,
"I like to think jellyfish
are the center
for our thoughts.
satellites for life
to be processed
and sent back
to us

in new codes,
each brain taking
on different memories:

the love,
the laughter,
the intimate,
the jealousy,
and the sorrow;

to piece us back
together again."

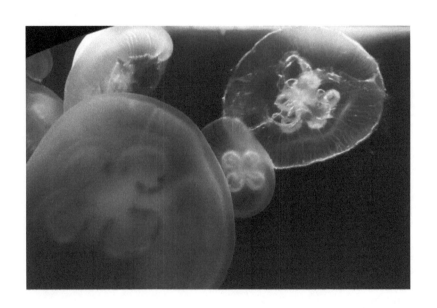

Instructions for My Former Self

In the attic
there is a box
made of tin
containing
storm clouds.

When you are ready,
you will sit in the attic
with your box of tin,
gripping lightning bolts
with your clenched fists
so hard--
you will carve four
waning moons
with your fingernails
into each of
your palms.

It is here
where you will realize
that holy hides
in melancholy.

Softly,
you will kiss
your open palms

on the waning craters.

When the craters
are kissed into your lips
they will fade
from your palms.

You will
become
full
with
the moon.
The storm clouds
will recede
into the box
made of tin.

And you will
know what it is
to finally
glow
in the dark.

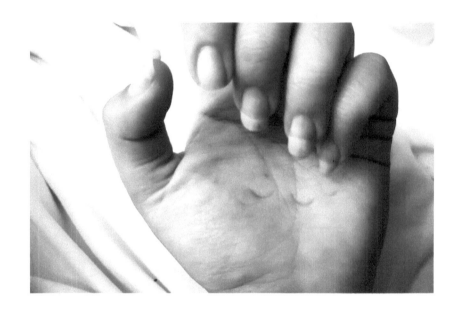

Kissing Toads

Hop came the toad.
He told me
"You are gorgeous."

He sang me punk rock lullabies
"Baby, baby, baby.
Won't you be my girl?"

So, I kissed the toad.

He became a punk rock boy.

I stayed a punk rock girl
but punk rock boy wanted more

so I learned to give up my thighs
before I was ready.
When my gift was too far in between.
I was replaced by faster girls
in back seats.

So, I never believed that fairy tales were meant for me.

So You Wander

"Everyone is in search of God,"
he tells me,
"in search of peace.
Salvation.
It's always a step ahead."

I can see *you* strutting the room.

He sees me flinch.
He tells me of glasses full.

I think of *you.*

Lips I can't get out of mind.

I imagine *you,*
spilling over
in my glass.

"There are thresholds for a reason,"
he says.

I still see *you.*

"I used to be able to read people a mile away."

I am closer than a mile,
I ask him,
"What do you see in me?"

"I stopped reading people.
People aren't for reading.
It's cheating.
What's the point of knowing
before you know?"

So, I try to put down my glasses.
Reading doesn't get you anywhere,
knowledge for the sake of knowledge,
for the sake of safety,
is not
where I want to be going.

I walk outside to the man
playing with fire.
I give the fire some spin.

Dangerous
is the most calm
I ever feel.

Calm always feels laced.
Like arsenic in the glasses,
filled with water wanting to spill.

Fire--
I know it will get me,
when it gets me.
I can see it.

"I used to stay away from storms," He says.

I never believed in that.
I always thought I'd find salvation after being struck by
lightning.
I've stood
in a lot of
open fields.

It's the walls
that make me feel unsafe.
Walls can come down.

He sees me flinch again.

Answered Prayers

I prayed for you
the night we met.

Weeks later,
I scribbled our ending
in a letter.

You carried it in your wallet.
Cracked it open
to see what a marvelous girl
you once knew.

I cursed you
for loving my surrender.
As if I had no part
in the breaking.

What a way I have,
to write myself
out of any life
I never actually
put the time to achieve.
Put it to rest
before it had any time to breathe.
As if satisfaction
lied in

being right
about the end,
rather than grateful
for the beginning.

I picked fights with you
over the way
you let me leave.

But you were
as right about me
as I was you.

Three degrees
to the left,
we could have
broken
each other.

Maybe
it was our aim
that was the problem.

Or maybe
we just knew more
about mercy
than we gave each other
credit for.

I never thanked God for you.

Waterfall Mantra

When the tears come
Let them be waterfalls
Until your throat dams you
and the falls dry up.

Then grab the pen,
the book,
the map.

For you have new territory
to chart
and wander.

The Princess Builds a Castle

The tarot reader says
"You need to be the princess."

I build a castle.

The hot dog man says
"Do not fall in love today."

I build a moat.

You tell me
"You are stunning."

I put barb wire around the tower
to see how far you climb.

When you reach me
I throw out my thighs
to distract you from all
the pain.

I pray against your hips
to ask me to slow down.

As you sleep,
I crawl out of bed to

ask the corner store clerk
how to love again.

He stares at me blankly
and hands me my cigarettes.

When you and I smoke them
I can't brake my tongue
long enough for you
to catch your breath
to ask about my castle.

You left exhausted.
I've been exhausted.

Beautiful Chaos

"You are
a beautiful chaos."

She strokes the hair off my face
as my head lays in her lap.

She kisses her palm
places it on my chest.

I etch 'A beautiful chaos'
on my left arm.

'Take As Is. As Is Take.'
across my collarbones.

A man reads my skin
as an invitation
to take.

Puts a pill in my drink.

For the night I am
a beautiful sleeping chaos.

In the morning,
I do not know where I am.

In the bath
I find his handprints
bruised into my thighs.

Love Me like the Sun Loves the Moon

You talked about the sun dying for the moon to shine.
You said you could love me like that,
all death and violence
as you handed me your grandfather's knife to protect
myself.

"Which punk rock couple could we be?"
You asked.

"Kurt & Courtney
or
Sid & Nancy?"

I cheekily said,
"Well, Courtney killed Kurt."
Your teeth unfurled as you reminded me,
"Sid killed Nancy."

I didn't know you were proposing a dare
for us to love like a knife fight.

What you didn't know
was that the sun
is no martyr.

No theatrics of love and violence could keep me.

I never offered you my freedom,
nor did I want yours.

You
didn't understand that the sun bows
for the moon to present her beauty.

Their love
is not one of sacrifice
or violence.

They extend themselves to each other.

Some days,
you can see them
share the same sky
and watch her
peak over clouds
to watch him bow down.

Each of his goodnight kisses
illuminates her.
He does not hold the moon
to be anything more than
herself.

Cherishing each wave she causes.

I wish I told you I wanted to be neither.
I wish I didn't accept the knife.

Knife fights

When I could no longer give you what you wanted
you drank and drank.

When I could no longer give you what you wanted
your grips became harder.

When I could no longer give you what you wanted
you tried to conquer.

When I could no longer give you what you wanted
you busted down the bathroom door.

When I held up the knife you gave me
you took it from me.

When I held up the knife you gave me
you became a dragon.

When I held up the knife you gave me
you underestimated how free I would be.

When it was all over
I vanquished the dragon.

When it was all over
I was told you wanted to control my fire.

It is all over
and I no longer believe in
living in castles.

Sincerely, Rum

I.　　　　Strangers will both lie and tell you the most
honest thing they ever said, if the rum hits right and the
topic of love sprouts between swigs of shared cups. These
half-truths are wishes of the way things were—something
sweeter than this. The stray dog that followed me around
the small Cuban town of Trinidad lay beneath my bench
never asking for treats, just the kindness of my eyes. The
two couples on the bench, in front and to the right of me,
laughed and gawked. They asked me if that stray was
really mine. I said he just follows me and that I call him
"little fox." This pleased them and they offered up a taste
of their rum.

II.　　　　I am honest in sentiment, but I paint broad
abstract strokes at boring questions such as "where are you
from?"—those details blur anyway. "I live in Mexico City,"
I tell them, and hide my accent that gives me away as US
born and bred. "Mexico, lindo y querido!" I coo, echoing
what most Cubans had responded to my origins. We toast.
The men ask me how it was possible that my boyfriend
would let me travel so far away. They paw at how free I,
truly, am. I say that I am not owned and that my boyfriend
fully trusts me and supports me. It is the honest wish—to
be trusted and not owned. Boyfriend, on the other hand, is
a strong word. It's been years since I've allowed someone
to get that close. Here lies the pleasantries of broad strokes,

to tell someone you're single invites too many compliments that they seem like lies.

III.   One of the men asks me to sit next to him and instructs his girlfriend to fetch us cigarettes so I can have a better taste of Cuba. They ask me what tacos are like and why Mexican movies always have men that shoot guns without ever getting shot or running out of bullets. I only know about tacos, personally, but I say that it's because Mexicans are "Muy chingón." They laugh and tell me that chingón means fuckers to them. I crack a side smile and say, "that too, sometimes."

IV.   I'm on my fifth shot of rum and I learn their love stories. The man who had his girlfriend fetch the cigarettes professes his love for her while she rolls her eyes. He is enchanting. He says he can do magic and that she was his assistant who fell in love with him despite him being 24 years her senior. She rolls her eyes at this and shakes her head no. He tells me he will do a magic trick to send me to my boyfriend. I reject the proposal, saying, "magic scares me and what if I come back with no pants?" Really, I'm scared of nothing to be sent to. He says he'll make flowers fall for me and the one I love, and hops on the bench reaching for the white flowers hanging above me. He told me I must take them to "my love."

V.   We take pictures.

VI.   The other couple leaves. I learn she is not his wife. I learn she is one of three other lovers.

VII.   The girlfriend hardly talks to me. She is not jealous. Her crossed legs before her and her arms spread across the bench signal she is not a woman as well-loved as the previous theatrics painted. She is with someone more in love with the thought of love than with her. She resents this. She says she will go buy a coke.

VIII.   I am left on the bench with the man. He tells me I am "lovely." I thank him for the flowers meant for "my love." He smiles and nods. He asks if he can speak to me honestly. I nod my head. "That's not my woman," he tells me. I don't jump at this. I already know. He tells me his woman is 19 years old and that after their public fight he called that girl up from another town, they been lovers for years. He asks me for my advice. I am 24 years old and I still have problems with currency exchange rates—simple mathematics. I have not been able to love, unconditionally. I know too well how to kiss someone without meaning it, in hopes it'd take everything else away like being heartsick over failed romance or just sheer boredom. I muster enough to say that "Love is difficult and that if he can call someone else up so fast, maybe he didn't really love his woman." I don't know if that is really true. It's hard to see how I've licked my own wounds from this high up. I tell him, "Passion is a beast that we mistake for love." He tells me the sex with the 19-year-old is different. I don't doubt this.

IX.   "Tell me more about how you love your boyfriend. How do you know you love him?" I paint him the sincere things said in between sheets. The long stares I have experienced. He is entranced. I tell him the last beautiful thing ever said to me and how I fit like a glove with him. His eyes shine capturing every drip. "You are the most sincere person I have ever met." I thank him. "But you do not love him," he says. I don't break eye contact. I don't dispute. I ask him why he says that. "It is because you do not suffer." I say pretty things again. Things I have felt in moments so light at 4AM between poetry and songs and sex. "Love isn't suffering. Passion is." I retort. The man keeps staring into my eyes. He searches past my sincerity for the truth. He cannot find it. He cannot find that I love too much—too many things. That I know everything is fleeting and I generally let things go without a fight; that my biggest fear is that I am a great lover that will never greatly love or be greatly loved. When his gaze drops, he asks where his girlfriend went, then asks if I need help getting home.

X.   We do not find her. We walk towards the same direction, three feet apart. We part two blocks from my momentary home. When I reach my room, the flowers are already dead. A dull ache rises. The streets ring with Cuban music and I can no longer stare at these dead flowers. I drop them into the bathroom trash can and start to pack for the next city.

Creation

The women take me to the woods.

Pound on drums.

They thunder.

I drink from a canister.
I savor
gasoline on my lips.

I swallow
lit matchsticks.

Fire
dances behind my pupils.

My body
pulsates orange.

Flames
crawl out of
the corners of my lips.

Firebreather

My uterus feels of ash,
my belly of burnt out matchsticks
and cluttered cigarette butts.

I used to like sharing a flame with someone.
They used to say it was "good luck."
In old time movies,
a cigarette lit
meant a time to flirt
and they say,
"Pretty girls don't light their own cigarettes."
so I almost never did.
There's this coy thing I do
with a flicker in my eyes and a half turned up smile.

I wanted to kiss you.
I wanted my lips to yours,
just to breathe you in.

Something about inhaling you
felt romantic.
It's like I thought my uterus
would feel less like ash.

I have been beautiful to many.

With a slight of hand, I say,
"This is what is ugly, but no fear!
Abracadabra!
This is what is beautiful."
People clap in awe.

Men want to touch me after that.
They want to kiss my lips.

I get to say "yes"
and I get to say "no."

I used to say "no" a lot less than I do now.

Not you, though.
You would nod your head.
You found me interesting
and I didn't know why.
It wasn't for my coy looks.
It wasn't for the center stage.

So, I didn't want to be the magician anymore.
I wanted to be the firewalker again.
No more parlor tricks.
I wanted to turn myself inside out
and show you charcoal.
I wasn't cheap tricks.
I knew what burning was like.
I have carried wildfires inside.

Here are all the matchsticks
I swallowed to prove it.

I took you for a firebreather.

A part of me thought you would smile
and you would dust off the ash.
Maybe,
you would turn inside out
and show me where the wildfire began,
how you
put them out,
and what you do
to play with the wildfires.

I wanted us to be inside out
and dancing with fire
in the forest.
So
I turned myself inside out
and put my feet to the coals
and said "Abracadabra"
so you would know it was time to clap.

"Abracadabra.
Abracadabra…
A-bra-ca-da-bra."

I was on repeat.

My feet were on fire.

You circled the ashes,
sipped the whiskey,
and nodded.

I wanted to turn myself back
outside again.
Turn myself back.

I thought you were a firebreather.

I thought you would breathe out the fire.
I could sense you were a firebreather.

I couldn't have been wrong.

But you never spit out the whiskey. You never set your
lips to the flame. You just kept taking in.

You are not the firebreather.

But I couldn't be wrong.

Maybe if I showed you more fire.
Maybe then you would know you are a firebreather.

Maybe then you can turn yourself inside out.

Because I couldn't have been wrong.

I didn't turn myself inside out for someone who didn't know how to see me.

I couldn't possibly have...

I was warned you were the devil.
That I was looking at the wrong fires.
That you rested among firepits
and you would take me away from my work.
You would be temptation.

But I couldn't have been wrong.

You needed to know you were the firebreather.
You told me you weren't the devil.

I tried to show you to breathe fire. How to walk with wildfire. You don't remember those parts. You kept drinking the whiskey.

You thought I doubted you.
I thought I believed in you too much.

And then it came that you spat out the fire.
You drank the whiskey

and spat out the fire.
You turned yourself inside out
to say you were nothing.

Your fire show was messy.

I tried to contain my fire,
I'd only let the smoke come out.
I burned inside.

More ash.

Maybe you thought I was the devil.

I stood on the coals.
I didn't turn inside out.
I burned inside.

I can't dance with the fire
if you spit it on my feet.

I didn't want to teach you to aim wiser
if you couldn't dance with me.

So, I say the fire needs to go out.

I am smoke inside.

You still wanted to see me

dance on the fire.

You told me to be well.

I become more ash.

I wanted the rebirth that came with the dancing.
I didn't want to try to burn each other down.

You spat on my feet.

You didn't dust off the ash.

I thought you were the firebreather.

For the Love of Frida

Encased in porcelain,
I unclench my limbs
to kiss water.

Encircled,
I peek
through the surface.

I am an island chain.

Water muffles the silence.

My eyelashes splashing,
hair adrift around me.

I gulp for air,
I try to stay still,

I cannot
yet breathe
underwater.

I am not ready
to breathe
underwater.

Horrendous gurgles
of water uncurl
from my curves.

I stay still.

I become a continent
with a whirlwind
between my feet.

The Ghosts are Alright

Your ghost
passed me.

I dodged his glare.

It's been six months
and I have seen no more ghosts.

There is no trace of
you,
yet
you
linger
in the pit of my stomach.

I don't want to say
I miss you,
more often
I want to say
I hate you
but we both know
I've never been good at lying.

I sit still
around the memories

of you
maybe
they won't touch me
if I do not flinch.
Maybe
they will fly
past me.

But memories
are not bees,
despite them
both
holding this world together.

The Honey Bees Couldn't Take Me

I tempt bees to swallow me.
I dip myself in honey
hoping they will take me,
pick me apart
and I will learn to bloom.

I leave sticky
and stung.

So, I take my sadness and feed you poems.
And you take your sadness
and feed me your poems.

We rinse off the sadness long enough
to think we can actually work.

You make a portrait of me
never knowing the whole of my nature,
send me the photo
but your brother sits on the portrait
and you never feel like fixing it.
I see your true nature.

When you come to see me
all we do is prove that two lonely people
can't fix each other's sadness.

It takes you over a year to tell me when it was that you
realized you could never love me.
Far harsher than how I tell you
that I love you
but I'm not in love with you.

And our sadness meets again.
If we are honest about why it didn't work,
maybe it can work?

I don't think you ever know how many times I leave your
side crying
I don't know if you know how badly I am starving.
You can hold me all night long
but the sadness always wins you out
and while you are my refuge
I am your cloud.

And the thing that sticks
is that it was
overwhelming.

Surrender

I walk into the open water
to look for the jellyfish.

I walk into the open water to beg them
to get these memories out of me.

To please start over.

Anything
but these memories.

Far from shore
the waves take over.

Far from shore
I swim harder.

I see the jellyfish
But cannot reach them.

The salt water stings my eyes.
My legs cramp.
I swallow the sea
and cannot breathe.

The panic
just let the waves

get the better of me.

I am tumbled
and I am bruised.
Saltwater in my veins.
Dimming my flames.

I give into the waves.
They do not take me.
They calm down enough to
cradle me back to shore.

I surrender
to the jellyfish dreaming.

The Prayer

Two women arrive at my door
in the rain.

They don't ask me to convert to their religion.
They just ask me if I want to pray for someone in my life.

They take my hands
"Who would you like to pray for?"

"Myself."

"What do you want?"

"Serenity."

Tulips

On the front porch,
a flowerpot
grows two tulips
amongst cigarette butts
we leave behind.
I call
the tulips
Hope
and
Soul
as they sprout
through our
refuse.
I feed them
caramels
and sing them
to sleep.

When you don't
call on my birthday,
I pluck
the cigarettes
from the flowerpot
and wander
the streets
looking for

testaments
that we didn't give up
so easily.

On my path,
two homeless men
ask me for
cigarettes.
I give them
the plucked-out cigarettes
from the flower pot
and they turn
to doves.

Cooing me a
birthday song,
they pick me up
drop me
on your porch
where you stand waiting,
palms up,
holding two tulips
you call
you
and
me.

Poor Fuckers

The storm subsides.

Sidewalks are
littered with dead birds,
all passed
mid-flight,
trying to get out of here.

They were struck down.

Something
took the life
right out of them.

Poor fuckers--
never stood a chance.

I step
around their corpses
into the blue house
with a party inside.
The guests didn't seem to notice
all the dead birds

outside.

Then he walks in,
smile
charming.

Our eyes hook.

It was far too long
since we had last
seen each other.

He approaches.
He didn't seem to notice
all the other guests inside.

Rain patters against
the window behind us,
as we sit side by side
on the pastel yellow couch.

His hand
stretches
into my lap
as he says,
"It's a shame
we stopped talking
to each other."

He inches closer.
He searches my gaze.

[crack]

A black crow
crashes
into the window
behind us.

His hand retreats.
His eyes unhook.

I pull his face back in
and whisper,
"Animals
can sense danger
before we do."

The Palm Reader

The palm reader takes my hand
and says,
"you have no love line."

The palm reader takes my hand
and says,
"Never mind it's there.
It's shattered."

The palm reader takes my hand
and says,
"You will have many loves."

The hot dog man says,
"Do not fall in love today."

The shell reader says,
"Find your inner child again
and you will find love."

The man says,
"I realized I could never love you."

The man says,
"You're stunning."

The man says,
"I want to love you."

The heart says,
"Fucking love me."

I lay and say,
"Just don't hurt me."

I lay and say,
"I don't know how to stop giving."

I crawl and say,
"I'm trying."

I sit and say,
"I'll love myself more."

I sit and say,
"I'll love myself more."

I sit and say,
"I'll love myself more."

I get up and say,
"This is me loving myself more."

The runes reader says,
"You are protected."

The palm reader takes my hand
and says,
"Howl more at the moon."

The palm reader takes my hand
and says,
"All I see are tulips."

The palm reader takes my hand
and says,
"Varinia, you are doing it."

Rorschach Test

She catches me staring at
her ink-blotted forearms.

"It's a Rorschach test,"
she says,
"what do you see?"

I cup her arms in my hands
and trace the blots.

"A woman
running
with wolves,"
I say.

Her eyes glimmer,
teeth unfurl.

She draws in
my left arm,
her fingers sniff
my tattoo
of the woman
staring at the moon.

She howls.

The Tattooed Man

When he talks about my perfection
I feel my pedestal rising.
I am drunk off the words
and still starving for bread crumbs.

I dream of lives that aren't our own.

With him,
I feel fire.
Without him,
I have nightmares of how
he will leave.

I don't tell him about the dreams
nor the nightmares.
I just listen to sad songs.
Hoping each exchange of "babe"
will hold us in place.

When I say it is
too good to be true
we both play the part
of who we think the other
wants us to be

and so comes his last act:

to need me
and never appear,
to just
disappear

and yet,
my panic doesn't come.
I do not shed a tear.
I am released of dreams
and nightmares.

So, I crack open my belly
to find the ash
has turned to tulips.

And I turn myself inside out
to roll in the lush field of flowers.

Imperfect and full
off my own tulip wine.

The Bullet Boomerangs

Four months pass,
the tattooed man
thanks me for showing him poetry.

Four months pass,
And he says
"I was a coward."

Four months pass,
And he says
"I made bad choices."

Four months pass
and I say
"You cannot lick your wounds here."

Honey

You call me "honey"
and I think it's an accident.

You called me "honey," again
and I think it's a joke.

You called me "honey," again
and I wonder if I am really sweet enough for the word.

I am a dear in the headlights.

My heart does not stop.

The calmness is foreign.

Guide

You guide me to the ocean
and I squeal at how cold it is.

You take my hand
and we walk further.

We are children in the water.

I do not fear the waves.

I do not leave you to search for the jellyfish.

I let the coolness take over.

The waves just play.

When they get too big
you lift me up.

For the moment that you are gone.
The waves tumble me to shore
and this time I laugh uncontrollably.

And the saltwater kisses
heal up all the wounds.

And bits of the ocean stay in your eyes

mixed with honey
when you look at me at night.

I Grew Up

I grew up on late night sounds of muffled fights
I grew up on pistachio shell dreams of beaches
I grew up on never enough
I grew up on poetry and liquor
I grew up on cigarettes and lust
I grew up in a castle with a moat and barbed wire fences
I grew up to give what I didn't want taken
I grew up to plan protection
I grew up to pink bedazzled butterfly knives
I grew up on loving like a knife fight

I've grown up on breaking down
I've grown up on flowers and the moon
I've grown up on crying inappropriately
I've grown up on kissing palms and laughing
uncontrollably
I've grown up on portraits of friends
I've grown up on not planning good-byes
I've grown up on getting out of puddles
I've grown up on choosing more wisely
I've grown up on swimming with the waves
I've grown up on asking more questions
I've grown up on magic
I've grown up on jellyfish dreaming

The Question

I chain smoke in front of him,
Each puff a wish to float out of this moment,
The nighttime sky tempting me to escape.

I cannot take flight,
The tulips blowing in my tummy,
begging me to stay.

I replay everything I had ever did wrong.
Every He that did me wrong.

I cough up a petal.

"I would like you in my life."
He says.

The cigarette doesn't even taste good.
It's a way to catch my breath.

Another petal falls out of my mouth,
The moon gets brighter,
The air more silent.

"What do you think God collects?"

I ask him.
He reaches for the petal,
Takes a deep breath,

"Relationships."

To-Do List

Water the flowers.

Howl at the moon.

The tulips keep growing.

Varinia Rodriguez handed you a feather, took your hand, and turned it into a penny. You called your mom that night and she told you she was proud of you. Every time you feel alone, you find the penny in your pocket, and remember to love yourself more. Sincere and intense, she embraces all the possibility to add meaning to life. Poet and photographer, she sharpens up the contrast of her surroundings and gives it new life. She heard that home is where the heart is and so she's been on a journey of finding her heart. If you've seen it, please tell it that she is on her way.

Photo Credit: Ale Kelly